THE TROJAN WOMEN

Also available by Brendan Kennelly

The Penguin Book of Irish Verse (Penguin, 1970; 2nd edition 1981)
The Boats Are Home (Gallery Press, 1980)
Cromwell (Beaver Row, 1983; Bloodaxe Books, 1987)
Moloney Up and At It (Mercier Press, 1984)
Mary (Aisling Press, 1987)
Landmarks of Irish Drama (Methuen, 1988)
Love of Ireland: Poems from the Irish (Mercier Press, 1989)
A Time for Voices: Selected Poems 1960-1990 (Bloodaxe Books, 1990)
The Book of Judas (Bloodaxe Books, 1991)
Medea (Bloodaxe Books, 1992)
Breathing Spaces: Early Poems (Bloodaxe Books, 1992)

EURIPIDES'
THE
TROJAN WOMEN

A NEW VERSION BY
BRENDAN KENNELLY

BLOODAXE BOOKS

ISBN: 1 85224 240 X hardback edition
       1 85224 241 8 paperback edition

First published 1993 by
Bloodaxe Books Ltd,
P.O. Box 1SN,
Newcastle upon Tyne NE99 1SN.

Bloodaxe Books Ltd acknowledges
the financial assistance of Northern Arts.

Cover printing by J. Thomson Colour Printers Ltd, Glasgow.

Printed in Great Britain by
Cromwell Press Ltd, Broughton Gifford, Melksham, Wiltshire.

PREFACE

It's hard to say to what extent the writing of a certain kind of play leads one, directly or indirectly, to the writing of another. I felt, after I'd finished *Medea*, that I wanted to write another play about women. So many things had been left unsaid. They always are. Again I was drawn to Euripides, this time to *The Trojan Women*. Almost fifty years ago, I heard women in the village where I grew up say of another woman, 'She's a Trojan', meaning she had tremendous powers of endurance and survival, was determined to overcome different forms of disappoinment and distress, was dogged but never insensitive, obstinate but never blackscowling, and seemed eternally capable of renewing herself. And she did all this with a consciousness that seemed to deepen both her suffering and her strength. Over the years I've observed these qualities in various women in different towns, cities and countries.

Some scholars and critics refer to *The Trojan Women* as a passive play, more a stirring spectacle than a real drama. I re-wrote this version of Euripides' play many times; and as I re-wrote it I found that it became increasingly active, although the women's situation overwhelmingly said that they were passive victims at the whimsical mercy of their male conquerors. And yet, within that apparent passivity of victims, I increasingly found a strong, active, resolute and shrewd note. My problem was to convey this note of active resolution, so closely linked with seemingly utter hopelessness, in language that came in waves suggesting both the women's spirits and the sea itself. Again, as I re-wrote the play, the women became more and more real to me; it was this deepening sense of the reality of the various women that I found hardest to capture. A man is trapped in his own language. How could I find the words to let these women express the ever-deepening reality of their natures? Well, I tried.

I wasn't writing a hymn to heroic women although I believe a man might spend his lifetime praising certain women and count that life well spent. I tried to write an active drama exploring the complex reality of a few memorable women. It was their different kinds of intensity that I found most magnetic. This play tries to present those mesmeric intensities in a fit language.

BRENDAN KENNELLY

THE TROJAN WOMEN

Brendan Kennelly's *The Trojan Women* was first performed at the the Peacock Theatre, the Abbey Theatre, Dublin, on 2 June 1993. The cast at the first performance was as follows:

POSEIDON, *God of the Sea*	Birdy Sweeney
PALLAS ATHENA, *Goddess*	Helene Montague
TALTHYBIUS, *a Greek herald*	Martin Murphy
HECUBA, *widow of King Priam,* *mother of Hector*	Cathy White
CASSANDRA, *prophetess,* *daughter of Hecuba*	Fionnuala Murphy
ANDROMACHE, *widow of Hector*	Pauline McLynn
MENELAUS, *King of Sparta*	Sean Kearns
HELEN, *wife of Menelaus* *(taken by Paris to Troy)*	Ali White
CHORUS	Tina Kelleher
MUSICIAN	John Dunne
DIRECTOR	Lynn Parker
SET AND COSTUME DESIGN	Frank Conway
MUSIC DIRECTOR	John Dunne
STAGE DIRECTOR	Suzanne O'Halloran
ASSISTANT STAGE MANAGER	Micil Ryan

The play is set outside the ruins of Troy.

Battlefield after a battle. Walls of city at back, broken. Huts to right and left, at front, with chosen women to be taken away by the Greeks. HECUBA *is lying on the ground, asleep. Dusk of early dawn. The God* POSEIDON *dimly seen before the walls.*

POSEIDON. The war is over. When will another war begin?
    I'm a tired old god in an old, tired world.
    I've seen war piled on war, horror on horror, death on death.
    I've seen love too
    and I say this:
    Love will come to rule the world,
    that is, women will rule the world.
    Although what you're about to see
    might seem to say that women
    are the rags and tatters of humanity
    or, at best, the perks of war,
    women will rule the world.

    I know that. I know it in all my broken dreams.
    (Almost bemusedly.)
    Women will rule the world.

    When that day comes, I won't be as
    old and tired as I am now.
    Only good dreams can rejuvenate
    a weary god.

    I came up out of the sea.
    The cold, fearless freedom of the waves flows through me.
    I see people on the run from love,
    devoting themselves to slavery.
    They call it responsibility.
    Some people would make a slave of the sea,
    and poison it as they enslave it.

    I have good and bad dreams
    and I make things.
    I made that city.
    Look at it now! A ruin!
    Freedom laughed and prospered there.
    Then a horse, its belly packed with death,
    a big, lumpy, clumsy, magical horse
    nosed through the walls
    and captivated hearts

7

with the ease of a child
getting its way with an old man
too tired or charmed to resist.
Men surrender in an evening
what they have spent their lives defending.
The city's freedom died in one fiery night.

Freedom is like health –
you never know it until you've lost it.

Look at that city – a ruin!
A dream of freedom in smithereens!
Limp and weary soldiers, dazed with victory,
wait for a wind to take them home
to wives and children left so long ago
they must be strangers now.

There's no stranger quite so strange
as the stranger waiting at home,
no stranger like the stranger in the bed.

Home? Home is often where strangers go to behave
as if they knew each other.
After war, strangers go home.

A war will make familiar love
into the strangest thing in the world.
War turns truth to lies and makes lies true.
I see my city –
scattered rags at my feet,
blackened bits of timber after fire, black as shame,
a bag of rubbish ripped asunder by starving dogs.
This is where good dreams grow feeble and sick.
Sick dreams spawn the evil of the world,
the river runs through the city's body like a shock.
The river is women's cries.
Women hover at the edge of war,
women are the spoils of war.
War breaks old ways,
creates new slaveries, new choices,
tramples old established laws to pieces
like children's bodies under the hooves of horses.
Women are spared the shedding of blood
to warm chosen beds.

Even now, victorious Greeks are drawing lots for women.
The war is over. It is time for prizes.
There are women hidden in these huts,
prisoners, slaves, prizes, warm melting fertile prizes.

Helen herself is a prize.
The most dangerously beautiful woman
in the world is a prize.
And Hecuba is a prize.
She lies here at the city's gates
crying of wrongs that can't be spoken.
Her face is brave, her tongue sharp, her heart broken.
But was there ever such a spirit in a woman's body?
Hecuba will fight to the end
and beyond the end.
Even in slavery, she struggles to be free.
But now, she is a prize.
Who will win her?
Hecuba's daughter, Polyxena, is a prize.
Grabbed from life, she will stare at a grave.
Imagine that! Staring, always staring, at a grave!
Cassandra is a prize, a virgin
chosen, favoured, impassioned by her god.
She must go to Agamemnon's bed.
The girl-virgin and the old gore-soaked killer king!
All the ravings in her heart
all the whirling pictures in her dreams
all the storm-thoughts in her head
all the sweetly crazed sensations in her body
are nothing now.
The virgin must lie down
with that old bagful of sin and sperm and war and death.
She must be the plaything of Agamemnon's lust.

Men kill each other
stab each other's hearts
split each other's heads
and then the damned survivors
take women to their beds.
Through the mucky fields of blood
an old man rucks in murderous havoc,
slaughtering everyone between him and his prize –

a virgin in his bed, her blood
the end of all, and the beginning.
The old style is with us still:
Kill and love! Love and kill!

He turns to go. PALLAS ATHENA, *goddess, becomes visible in the dusk.*

And I, creator turned survivor, for I have learned
to survive my own creations,
must leave this city of my dreams,
this old broken city
that will always live in me.
My heart is only
smashed bits and pieces of my city.

PALLAS. Gentle Poseidon!

POSEIDON. Pallas Athena! Have you something to tell me?

PALLAS. I need a friend. Are you my friend?

POSEIDON. Do you pity
this old broken city?

PALLAS. Are you my friend?
Will you give me your helpful hand,
your strong mind?

POSEIDON. What have you to tell me?

PALLAS. I would give these Greek ships
a homecoming to remember.

POSEIDON. Your spirit is a knife.
The blade is hate and love and rage.
I see the knife in your eyes.

PALLAS. They wronged me
In my own holy place.
They have forgotten the obscenity
they committed against me.

POSEIDON. I know what Cassandra suffered
at the hands of Ajax. He dragged her off,
beat her, insulted her, ridiculed her body and mind.
How can a man who so humiliates a woman go unpunished?

PALLAS. Not a hand was laid on Ajax.
Not one Greek moved against him
as if the violence he'd inflicted on Cassandra
was nothing at all. These Greeks no longer
know the meaning of what they do.

POSEIDON. It was your hand
gave Troy to the Greeks.

PALLAS. My hand is ready to strike them now.

POSEIDON. My heart is ready to help your hand.
What's your desire?

PALLAS. A homecoming that means
they will never reach home.

POSEIDON. Never, never reach home?
You want to let them flounder forever?
You want them to be
lost and conscious forever in the sea
wandering, wandering, never to come
into the sanity of home? You want
all these ships, packed with victorious men,
to be lost, lost, never to be found again?

PALLAS. I want them to know that home
is what is always in the mind and always out of reach.
I want the sea
to be a sea of death
working for me.
I want you to make the sea
mad with its own ferocity,
wild with the genius of its treachery
till it grows thick and sluggish
with lost Greeks.
I want to see the day
when Greeks will speak my name
and know the meaning of the name they say.
Poseidon, make the sea my friend.
These Greeks have lost respect for me.
Maybe they'll find it again
at the bottom of the sea!

POSEIDON. I'll stir the sea to madness
    never known before
    until the bones of drowned men
    pile and thicken on the sea-floor.
    Bodies piled on bodies will litter every shore.
    Be on your way, your strength and pride
    deepen because heaven is on your side.
    Your triumph-time will come
    when the last ship leaves for home!

Exit PALLAS.

    How stupid you are, how blind
    all you who smash cities to the ground
    violate the holy places
    desecrate the graves of loved ones
    and vilify the honoured dead.
    All this you do, and more, and worse,
    and never ask why.
    Ask nothing, either, when it's your turn to die.

Slowly the day comes. HECUBA *wakes, looks about her.*

HECUBA. Lift my head! I will lift my head!

    This is not the beautiful city I have known.
    This is not the city whose every corner is part of me.
    This is not my home.

    I look, I look...I see...ruin, desolation, decay,
    my children lost, my land trampled, my man cut down,
    every shred of dignity a feather in the wind,
    every decent heart turned into idiot, fool and muttering clown.

    I watched over you, I watched...are you nothing at all?
    Is my heart twisted? My mind strayed?
    My words timid and weak?
    Where can I turn for help?
    Who will begin to listen to my voice
    when it dares to speak
    of pain in my bones, my flesh, my very blood?
    In this morning-light, my body rocks with pain
    caught in the rhythm of its cries,
    my own tears burning music out of my eyes,
    fierce cold burning music flowing far and wide

for what is lost, insulted, broken, ruined, dead.

Look at my city, look at my body,
this head, this neck, these hands, these lips, these eyes,
my city is lost, so is my country.
My body, heavy, waits, packed with the cries
of my dead husband, my dead children,
my dear dead friends.
My body waits – for what?
A man's eyes! A man's eyes will cover me,
examine me from head to foot.
A man's eyes
can look at me in public
as if I were his private property.
A man's eyes can say things to me
that his tongue would never dare to utter.
A man's eyes can be as bold
in the daylight streets of a city
as a knife in a killer's hand.
A man's eyes mock every rule and law
and scorn all decent boundaries.
A man's eyes can strip me naked in a way,
a lover's hands
would never know how to do.
A man's eyes can
rape me in the street
and not a single word need ever be said!
A man is going to look at me, his eyes will say –
I want you in my bed.
This man has killed other men,
this man is used to getting his way,
accustomed to winning:
winning is why he's alive.

He'll win me,
a prize, a trophy.
He'll wear me like a medal,
discard me like old skin.
Why not? The dead in the earth know
that such a man was born to win!

Yet, may not a woman
fight, yes, fight, here and now?

May not a woman
win?
How?

(She stares towards the Greek ships on the far shore.)

Ships! Ships!
Packed with merciless faces.
How did you find your way
into our holy places?
Over the waves you came
driven in savage joy
to mingle glory and shame
in the streets of Troy.

Ships! Why did you come?
For a woman? A woman:
the test of her maker's dream,
the test of all things human.
Havoc and death she brought
and ruin to me and mine
and she laughed in the eyes of men
as if her heart were divine.

As if her heart were divine!
And who am I...
Here at the door of a Greek king's house
with a heart that seems ready to die?
A woman without a home
riddled with grief for her dead
humiliation in her heart
confusion splitting her head.

(She gets up, calls to the other Trojan women in the huts.)

Women! Women! Come out! Come out!
It is time for you to make your cry.
Not the cry of men:
it is time for the cry of women now.
This is the cry that will deepen in time
never uttered till now, but uttered once
must be shrieked again and again.
This is the cry of a woman's soul
hitting the cities built by men
rocking the world from pole to pole.

A WOMAN *comes out from a hut. Others come out slowly, stealing out, afraid.*

FIRST WOMAN. Why do you cry like that?
    Deep in the hut
    I heard your sorrow pouring out
    in words that ripped and cut
    their way into my fear.
    Your sorrow and my fear
    tell me that we
    will never again be free.

HECUBA. The ships are moving on the shore.

SECOND WOMAN. The ships are coming alive.
    The ships are packed with our people's gold.
    The ships are waiting for us women.

THIRD WOMAN. What do the ships want?
    What will the ships do?
    Will they sweep us off as prisoners –
    You, and you, and you?

HECUBA. I don't know. Contain yourself. You mustn't be
    the victim of your fearful dreams.

FIRST WOMAN. We will be prisoners, slaves,
    even now the grinning ships
    prepare our doom.
    They sail by their arrogant star
    and mock at all we are.
    Women, come out of your tents!
    Come out and see the ships
    that will take you to slavery.
    COME OUT! COME OUT!

HECUBA. Do not wake Cassandra!
    God has maddened her.
    Conquering men will mock her.
    Let me never witness that ridicule.
    My city, O my city,
    you are broken-lonely
    and broken-lonely these men would have us go
    to places we can't begin to know.
    Do not wake Cassandra! She is driven out of herself

15

because God has breathed into her blood
something of his own sorrow at the devastation
caused by murderous men who want us now as prizes.

Other women come out.

FOURTH WOMAN. Dear Queen, I steal out of the tent
of the Greek King.
I steal, fearful and trembling.
You called. Why did you call?
Am I to die? Are we to die?
What is the meaning of your cry?

FIFTH WOMAN. The cries are coming from the ships,
the ships' cries must be heard,
every word a tyrant
on the lips of tyrants.

HECUBA. No. Look! It is the morning light,
strong, unstoppable and bright.
The day and all it brings of good and bad,
is yours and yours alone.
Women, although our hearts are grieving,
we are the light of morning.

FIFTH WOMAN. I am cold and weak with fear.

SIXTH WOMAN. Someone in the distance. A Greek!
A Greek is coming this way.

FIFTH WOMAN. Whose slave am I?
Who has won me as a prize?

HECUBA. Easy, easy! Keep your peace.
They're drawing lots for us.
Keep your peace.

FOURTH WOMAN. Where will they take me?
To some island without a name
where I must lie
under the sun and moon of shame?
Never, never again to see
my own city.
Where will they take me?
I stand here,
I wait for some man's finger

to point at me.
No need for him to say a word,
his finger will say it all —
I want you!
I WANT – YOU!

Who will look at me like that?

HECUBA. Where will I be taken?
Into some nightmare den
where I can never sleep, never awaken?
Into some house of drunken, mocking men?
Shall I become a battered slave,
used a moment, dumped again
like a withered flower on my own grave?
Or must I rear my enemy's children
to sneer and spit in my ageing face,
I who grew in love and joy
proud and happy in this place,
a Queen in Troy.

A WOMAN. (*To* ANOTHER.) What will you do?

THE OTHER. The ships will cry.
I will be dragged into a ship.
Shall I live or die?
I have my fingers, lips, face, eyes.
If I live, may I be wise,
wise enough to see myself
as men see me,
to use my eyes as I see them use theirs.
When someone looks at me and says
I want you,
may I be wise enough to make him think
he is a winner born.
We are losers now.
We know what winners want.
They will pass us from one to the other
like dishes at a feast.
We are bread and meat and fish and fruit and wine.
They will eat and drink, drink and eat
again and again.

We live to satisfy the winners.
How shall I satisfy my winner?
With all I have, my body,
I am nothing but my body,
my body, my only weapon.

ANOTHER. I have my child, I see my child,
he looks at me as though
he can't believe that I should ever go
away. Away. Is my child enslaved or free?
The ships are crying in the sea.

ANOTHER. A lost child! A crying sea!
But there's worse, worse, waiting for me.
A Greek's bed, a sneering Greek's bed.
I would be free, free as the dead,
free of a body digging my body,
crying in the dark, lost and lonely,
longing for my city where my dreams of love began.

ANOTHER. God's curse on every rutting man!

ANOTHER. To serve some idle bitch
sprawled in the warm shade:
'What kept you? Slave, be quick!
Why have you delayed?
Why do you shiver like a rat
before boiling water scalds its throat?
Fetch me a drink! Prepare my bed!
My man wishes to rut.'

ANOTHER. Maybe I'll find a gentle place,
A kind hand, a kind face...

ANOTHER. But not a scurrilous loud house
where lewd voices bully us
with vicious, stupid jokes
and stupid, vicious words
and horrid laughter raining down
on our pain.

ANOTHER. Here comes a Greek from the ships;
the usual arrogant air,
triumphant set of the lips.
What news does he bear

for us who are slaves from now on?
We are the booty of men,
prizes the Greeks have won!

TALTHYBIUS, *with soldiers, enters.*

TALTHYBIUS. Hecuba, you know me: Talthybius.
I bring news.

HECUBA. Women, you are looking at our fear.

TALTHYBIUS. The lots are cast, Hecuba, the lots are cast.
Lives and loves are won and lost.

HECUBA. What man? What land? What heart? What head?
What hill? What glen? What house? What bed?

TALTHYBIUS. Each woman has her own road to travel,
her own cup to swallow,
her own bed to sleep in.

HECUBA. What is our fate?

TALTHYBIUS. You must ask about each woman in turn.

HECUBA. Cassandra?

TALTHYBIUS. She is Agamemnon's prize.

HECUBA. What?

TALTHYBIUS. Yes, Cassandra sleeps in the King's bed.
Her body burns and cools at his will.
It's her good fortune the King has favoured her.

HECUBA. Polyxena?

TALTHYBIUS. Your daughter?

HECUBA. Yes.

TALTHYBIUS. She must watch Achilles' tomb.

HECUBA. My daughter? To watch a tomb?
What can this mean?
What is the reason for this?

TALTHYBIUS. Your daughter's happy.
She has nothing to fear.

HECUBA. How is she? Where is she? What is she doing?

TALTHYBIUS. She watches Achilles' tomb.
That is all she does, all she must do.
One thing alone, one solitary duty
consumes the heart and mind of your Polyxena.
Your daughter's eyes must stare at the earth
where dead Achilles lies. That is all.
Staring at death is her life's work.

HECUBA. Andromache?

TALTHYBIUS. She belongs to Pyrrhus, Achilles' son.

HECUBA. How quickly women are lost
when wars are won.

TALTHYBIUS. So much killing must bring some profit to someone.

HECUBA. (*Pause.*) Whose slave am I?
To whom do I belong?

TALTHYBIUS. Odysseus, King of Ithaca.

HECUBA. Odysseus! Tricky, slithery Odysseus!
A liar, sharp and pitiless,
is Hecuba's master.
Odysseus! No man on earth
has such scorn for justice.
Everything Odysseus says and does
means one thing:
every action, oath, right and wrong,
even the hate of his lying tongue
works to advance the tricky art
of his false and twisted heart.
Where men and women make love, Odysseus makes hate.
He is the crookedest creature in the world.

My master!

Women of Troy, cry for me now.
Cry for Hecuba this black hour.
You may fare badly but at least
you will not sleep with this beast.

FIRST WOMAN. Hecuba, you know your fate.
But who is the new owner of my life?

TALTHYBIUS. Men, go fetch Cassandra. Bring her here

As quickly as you can
I will give her to the King
And give these other women
To the men who're waiting for them.
What's that? What's that? There! There!
What is that light? A fire!
These women are setting fire to themselves!
They're setting fire to their own bodies
rather than go to our waiting ships.
Quick! Quick! Bring the women out.
If this fire puts women's bodies
beyond the pleasure-loving reach of men
the King's rage will burn my head.

HECUBA. There is no fire.
It is a body all alight with the breath of God.
It is Cassandra.

Enter CASSANDRA, *in white, a great torch in her hand, a garland on her head. She does not see othe others.*

CASSANDRA. I am going to be a bride. A bride!

Lift high the flame
I give this flame to God
I praise God's name
in field and sea and flower and cloud.

Lift high the flame
soon I shall be wed
a happy bride
blessed and loved in a king's bed.

Why are you crying?
A father dead? City on fire?
I go garlanded,
young bride of desire.

Lift high the flame
this torch is borne with pride
a girl sleeps her last sleep.
Enter a bride.

I offer fire to God
His fire lives in me
His fire fills a woman's love
with God's intensity.

I bid myself to live
as I have not lived before,
I bid myself to dance
over my father's bones.

Let me dance like sunlight now
where my dead father lies,
dance O my dancing feet
dance like the dancing skies

dance like the happy light,
let earth and heaven sing
here where I make this bright
and fiery ring.

(She makes a circle round her with the torch and visions appear to her.)

Is it you? How beautiful your face,
your eyes, your mouth, your brow.
Hear my prayer, please
be with me now.

Is it you? Am I still alone?
O laugh and dance with me.
Be the fire unknown to men.
Dance, dance eternally.

Come, praise the marriage-God,
greet him with songs of pride.
When the songs are scattered like dust,
still praise the bride.

Praise me, women, praise me now
and cry for the heart and head
of the man who must take me
into his bed.

FIRST WOMAN. She is out of herself.
Hold her, hold her tight, down,
or she'll run to the ships.

HECUBA. O my Cassandra,
        woman, child, woman,
        why do you ring yourself with savage fire
        and speak wild words of impossible desire?
        Your torch, your leaping, dancing torch
        is far from the old dream of peace.
        But this is what is.
        You are the child and prize of war.
        You know what the man said:
        killing and death and howls of agony
        are the pathway to our marriage-bed.
        Give me that torch; it bears
        nothing of the old, holy fire
        and your frenzy will not restore it.
        What can a woman learn from her grief?
        If she is lucky, she will endure
        and in enduring, pick up shreds of wisdom.
        Women, take away this torch.
        And now, on dear Cassandra turn your eyes.
        Look at her. What is her fiery dance?
        What is the music of her fiery cries?
        (Taking the torch, she hands it to a woman.)

CASSANDRA. I will lie in Agamemnon's bed.
        I will kill Agamemnon.
        I will set his house on fire
        as he set mine.
        Out of his burning body
        out of his burning house and bed
        my father and my brothers
        will come from the dead.
        Whoever loves me against my will
        teaches me how to kill!

(She checks herself. Then she goes deeper into herself.)

Let me go into my ecstasy.
        Do not hold me from my ecstasy.
        I must go down, down
        into the pit, beyond the pit
        of human darkness
        to find my special light.
        I will find my special light.

I will go down, down
beyond the dreams of murderers
beyond the murderer's blood on the black axe
beyond the black axe sunk in the bottomless swamp
beyond the thoughts of horror that are half-stopped by fear
beyond the girl raped in the whimpering laneway –
I will go down through that appalling night
to find my special light.

Already, I know something.

You and I and these women
are happier than the Greeks, our conquerors.
The power of God is in me.
Do not hold me from my ecstasy.
Let me tell you this.

One woman's beauty is the death of countless Greeks.
And what is the achievement of their King?
He killed love that hate might live.
He will die from dead love and living hate,
a conquering, strong, caricature of a man
who never began to know himself.

The power of God is in me.
Listen.

Thousands of Greeks struggled and fought
bravely. Thousands of these thousands died.
For what? Those who died
will never see their children.
No wife came to prepare them
for the grave;
they lie here, all here,
in this foreign, angry earth, this earth that hates
their dead, decaying bones.

At home the same sad story:
women waited, died lonely,
old men longed for sons
who are but poor accursed bones
in nameless, unattended graves,
bad patches of earth
not worthy of a beggar's spit
or the stench of a dead dog in the sun.

These are the things the Greeks have won.
These are the prizes of conquering men.
Men who win wars win nothing.

Listen.

Now, I speak of us.

We are a fighting people
and fighting we died to save our people.
In the mad rage of war
friends bore their dead friends home.
Women's hands washed them,
wrapped them in white shrouds
to lie at peace in their own loved earth.
And while the gentle dead enjoyed
a sweet eternal sleep
their living friends fought on
knowing what they were fighting for
close to their wives and children
in their own land, passionate, at home,
not like the Greeks,
the lost, conquering, joyless Greeks.

And Hector, our dead hero, what is his grief?
Hector is dead, Hector is true and proud
and we all know the great heart he had.
That knowledge is a gift from the Greeks.
Years ago, we hardly knew Hector
or the courage that was in him
but now we know the truth of his blood,
a man loved by his people, loved by his God.

Listen. God is in me. Listen.

People of my heart, do everything you can
to banish war
from the lives of women, men and children.
But if war comes to the land
like a murderous brute into your house
and you find that you must fight
the fight like people who have found
their special light,
there's no evil in that fight.

Therefore, my mother, do not pity the dead
of this great-hearted city.
And do not pity me,
bride of a conquering King.
He'll swell with royal pride to sing
my praises and my charms
locked in his hot, majestic arms.
It is his death
that I will sing.
Love will kill a king, and kill a king, and kill a king.
When he governs me in bed
shall I pray for words to praise him right?
Shall I whisper and sigh and cry in passion?
Or shall I lift the black axe out of the swamp?
Shall I wipe the bloodstains from the blade?
Shall I become the black axe
in my mind, in the bed
where Agamemnon rides me in the dark
or in the light?

Randy Agamemnon! Godalmighty fucker Agamemnon!
You are making love to a black axe
covered in bloodstains,
and the black axe feels like the flesh of a woman
chosen to pay homage to your greatness.
Her only problem is to pay that homage right.
Listen, Agamemnon, listen!
Look into my eyes, Agamemnon, look into my eyes:
the war is over, you are the winner, I am your prize.
While you are loving in the dark or in the light
the black axe is singing of your death.
Agamemnon! Listen in the silence of your tired fucker's body
to the song of the black axe.

TALTHYBIUS. (*Breaks the spell she has cast.*)
If I did not know that you are mad,
maddened by the thought
that you must share Agamemnon's bed,
like it or not,
I'd make you swallow your wild words
here and now.

Why in the name of all that's holy,
in the name of hard-won victory,
did Agamemnon choose such a mad creature,
such a perversion of woman's nature?
Yet he has! He has!
My King! My master has chosen
a mad woman before all other women.
Your madness sparks a madness in my King.
Who are you? Where do your words come from?
What do they mean?
Look! I will forget all that you have said!
I will forget every word of praise and blame,
the hate you generate at Agamemnon's name,
I will forget it all.
Come, walk with me. Walk in peace with me,
I'll take you to Agamemnon.
And heaven grant that he may find in you
what he believes he will!
Do the Gods play mocking tricks when Kings pick women?
I'm only a common soldier
a poor man
but I'd never be so daft
so clean out of my head
as to choose a lunatic like this
to share my bed!

(*He pauses, looks at her.*)

Crazy! Crazy! Is Agamemnon crazy too?
Or will he get a special kick
out of fucking a lunatic virgin like you?

(*Goes among women.*)

This creature's mad!
Are you all mad? Are all women mad?
Or are you crafty bitches
waiting to see how the wind blows
and what the sea will bring?

(*Begins to approach various women.*)

You! What's in your head?
You look beaten; but a beaten

woman still plays games.
Even lying in the dirt you
can turn up trumps!

You! What schemes are covered
by your helplessness?
You can't fool me!
You're as moody as the sea,
and as treacherous, if a man's not careful!

And you! And you! And you!
What plans have you?
Are you planning to go mad
so that you can distract a man?
Are you cultivating the lost look,
the hurt look, the beaten look,
the bruised and battered look?

(He turns to go, then speaks gently to HECUBA.*)*

When you are told to do so, go with the men
sent by Odysseus. I have heard
the Queen that you will serve
is a kind, wise woman.
I have heard
that all her thought is sweet and patient
and her ways are gentle.

CASSANDRA.
    (She sees him, the entire scene, for the first time.)
    (To TALTHYBIUS.*)* Slave! You poor, despicable slave
of a go-between!
What would you think
if you had a mind of your own!
What would you do
if you weren't the slave of another man?

    (To OTHERS.*)* Slaves! Mother! Voices of death!
The shadow of dead men's agony hovers over all,
the day wears pain like a black jewel
and I can smell the fingers of men
whose hands serve a King of hate.
Your voice is gentle to my mother.
Do you know what you are saying?

My mother must go to Odysseus?
My mother's place is not with Odysseus.
My mother's place is here. Here.

(To herself.)
Why do I speak?
Odysseus knows nothing of what waits for him.
His troubles have hardly begun.
A man astray, lost, betrayed,
here and there like a fish in the sea –
the man who plans to bed my mother!
Odysseus is going home.
For ten years he will struggle to go home. Home!
He will taste horror after horror
he will see his own men eaten alive
he will see his own men changed into pigs
he will be battered shipwrecked stupefied
he will see the healing light of the sun
become the voice of his own agony.
He will go to hell, alive to hell,
he will wander the sea
and when he reaches home at last
the door that he has longed to open
will admit him to appalling sorrow.
That is what faces the man
who plans his pleasure with my mother.

And what faces me?
Take me now! Take me to the King,
I shall lie beside the King
...lie beside the King!
King! Lump of dust and blood and muck,
I'll go to your bed.
But there's another bed I see for you –
in a hole somewhere in the ignorant hills
with icy rain forever spitting down.
Dead...outcast...naked as the winter light...
Who is it? – It is I
lying by my King.
All around, I hear them cry,
the wild beasts of the wilderness,
they move in slowly, crying, slowly,

hungry, crying, to where we lie
in bed. The wild beasts watch our bodies
and there from where I lie
beside this thing that calls itself a King
I study the wild beasts. How innocent they are!

(She grips her wreathed head.) Flowers! Flowers!
Flowers of my God breathing his love
into my blood until I feel
the old unkillable joy!
No man can humiliate me forever!

Hell! King of hell!
I'll tear every flower from my head
and pitch it to hell!
O God, these flowers…white, white,
darkness…there was a special light.
If any shred remains, be with me now.
White petal of my heart, be with me now.

(To TALTHYBIUS.) Take me to the ships!
I face the sea.
A man's body, important with the power of hell,
walks with me.
A man's body, a winner's body, waits for me.

Mother – Goodbye.
Goodbye, my city.
My sisters and my brother, goodbye,
Goodbye, my father.
No, I am with you all.
Goodbye. I am with you all.
(To TALTHYBIUS.) I am ready, slave!

She goes with TALYTHYBIUS *and soldiers.* HECUBA, *motionless a while,*
falls to the earth.

WOMAN. Help her!
Help the Queen from the ground!
Raise her up!

Women go to help. She brushes them off, and speaks from the earth.

HECUBA. Here…let me lie here.
Please, please, do not try to help me now.
I know what it means to be nothing,

I have heard voices of nothing call me
to their place of nothingness.
If I call on God for help
all I find is his helplessness.
Yet I must seek and I must cry
for help that seems not to exist.
O let me dream of things long gone
and feel the living presence of the past.
I knew great men, I walked with kings,
now I must lie in a hated bed.
Strong sons I had, the very best
and I was proud to mother them
and I saw them put to death
and I must lie in their killer's bed.

My daughters too! I reared them
for those randy, conquering Greeks.
Not a daughter with me now!
Not a shred of hope is left
that I shall look into their eyes
nor they in mine, ever again.
Women are swept by men who think
that conquest makes them half-divine.
Now I descend into the pit,
a captive slave at my enemies' feet
forced to do whatever they wish:
'Open the door! Shut the door!
Grind the wheat! Bake the bread!
Set the table! Sweep the floor!
Lie soft and warm and open your legs!'

A woman must be whatever
a conquering man wishes her to be!

To think that all my life I walked proud and free!

My clothes are torn, my flesh is torn,
humiliation chills my veins, my bones,
and I am sick with shame!

Think of it! Simply that I must lie
in a man's bed, waiting for his pleasure,
my soul repelled, my heart numb with terror,
my mind half-crazy with loathing.

Simply that I must submit
to what freezes my blood with hate,
think what seas have weighed on me,
have poured over me in their ecstacy
and will pour, pour
until I am no more...
And O my dear Cassandra,
daughter I have loved in a way
no music reaches, no word can say,
where have you gone?
What will you become?

And where are you, Polyxena?

And my dear sons, where are you?

How, in so short a time, can this
beautiful world become a world of loss?

And who can help me now,
lying on this ground?
What hope is there?
I am what I am, a slave
who once walked free,
an upright woman in her natural beauty.
But now, I am cast down,
stupid as a stone.

How shall I ever stand again?
I have lost so much
there is nothing left for me to save.
No human can be happy
this side of the grave.

WOMAN. If there's any music left in this world
it is the music of our grief.
Our grief was a huge horse,
his belly packed with death.
It was so beautiful, that horse,
huge and mighty and high,
young women left their homes,
so did all the old men.
Young and old sang and rejoiced in thanksgiving
for the huge beautiful creature
bringing their doom.

Men and women of our city put their eyes upon the horse
and pulled it after them
like a ship they were about to launch
until it stood
on the floor of the stone temple of Pallas Athena.
It stood there on the floor,
the floor that soon would flow with blood.
As the night descended
the people sang and danced
in the shadow of the horse.
Everywhere, torches flared in gratitude.
Even in the darkened houses
the rooms glowed with happiness and joy.
The people's hearts were glad:
had not heaven sent a special gift, a horse,
beautiful and big enough
to bear the weight of all their dreams
and sweep them forward to a future made of hope?
That night, I myself was singing in the choir
before the Temple of the Virgin in the Mountains
when suddenly the city rocked
with cries of havoc and despair
filling the bloody streets of massacre.
Out of the perfect, gigantic horse
Death poured like a black wave over the city,
the symbol of our hope became our doom,
the black wave swallowed everyone in its path,
old men froze in disbelief,
children were struck dumb with terror,
young women in their beds
knew that horror was upon them.
Their warm flesh was ice.
Since that night, the women of this city
have swallowed every horror
the conquering Greeks could dream of.
And believe me, these men dreamed and acted
with an energy so obscene
I ask myself, what is a woman?
How much abuse can a woman take,
how much horror can a woman endure
before she ceases to be a woman,

before she ceases to be human?
Will the day come when she won't be human?

WOMAN. No woman is anything now.
Women are dead. We are all dead
and being dead we may become
the grass that grows between stones.
Or we may become the tears
that you have cried in the past
for some inexplicable sense of waste,
some insult you suffered or threw
at some man in a public place
because he stared into your face
as if he'd know you in a way
you could never know yourself.

All women are dead of shame tonight
and being dead we may cry
for the suffering of our city,
for the hungry in our midst,
the lonely in our rooms,
the sprawled outcasts in our streets
the lost in doors and laneways,
the dumb in the pity of shadows,
the mad in the isolation of themselves.

Women, we are become this city,
we are become its untold loss,
its forgotten truths, commemorated lies,
its unspoken and unwritten history,
its guilty silences and echoing scandals,
its tiny gestures forgotten soon as made
its winters learning how to smile
its summers renewing the old chill
its mornings laughing
like girls thrilling to their first love.

What can our city ever be
but we
in this poverty
worse than death?

But they will bring us back from death –
our conquerors!

34

And we must go and lie with them –
our conquerors!
And we must be
the mothers of the children of our enemies.

Our children – the children of our enemies!

Who knows anything of love or hate
or joy or grief or callousness or pity?

All we know is that
we are our city.

Our broken, fallen, ridiculed city.

Enter ANDROMACHE, *with her son.*

WOMAN. Andromache!
Where are you going?

ANDROMACHE. To a Greek's bed.

HECUBA. One more hell
And one more woman in it!

ANDROMACHE. Your word describes my heart.

HECUBA. Hell is the air we breathe.

ANDROMACHE. You have yours.

HECUBA. Yes.

ANDROMACHE. You are lost – alone.

HECUBA. Yes. And my city is lost – alone.
And plundered.

ANDROMACHE. Most savagely raped.

HECUBA. Dead children.

ANDROMACHE. Shattered streets of sorrow.

HECUBA. These streets are me.

ANDROMACHE. I want my lover.
Give me my lover.

HECUBA. Your lover's dead.
His flesh is black earth,
not for your flesh now or ever.

35

ANDROMACHE. Protect me. Where is my love?

HECUBA. Where is my love? O my love
let me be with you, where are you,
O my love?

ANDROMACHE. I could lift my heart out of my breast,
search every corner of it
for one small sign
of love that lived there,
like my children in my house
so happy
I tremble to remember.

HECUBA. Do not remember. Do not remember.

ANDROMACHE. If I banish children from my head
A burning city flames instead.

HECUBA. I am criss-cross streets of fire.

ANDROMACHE. Dead men lie naked,
vultures croak for joy
because the criss-cross fiery streets
are the death of Troy.
Love staggers here and there,
raggedy flesh, mad eyes,
starved hands flailing the air
packed with cries.

HECUBA. Home! My home!
The end is come.

FIRST WOMAN. Can Hecuba cry?
Is she frozen within?

ANDROMACHE. What do you see?

HECUBA. I see God's hand
killing my land.

ANDROMACHE. Hooves of maddened cattle
are pounding my head.

HECUBA. We're helpless.
They've taken Cassandra.

ANDROMACHE. There's worse to come.

HECUBA. Is it possible?

ANDROMACHE. Polyxena is dead, her body
    thrown on Achilles' grave.

HECUBA. That's what Talthybius said,
    I didn't understand.

ANDROMACHE. I touched her body where it lay,
    I wept for her.

HECUBA. *(To herself.)* Beyond imagining!
    Beyond enduring!
    Who can imagine such evil?
    My daughter's body thrown on a Greek's grave
    like a flower in the gutter.

ANDROMACHE. Polyxena is dead, free
    of the misery where we are trapped.

HECUBA. Death is not life.
    Death is nothing, less than nothing.
    Life laughs at death.

ANDROMACHE. Better to be dead
    than living horribly.
    To be dead is to be
    beyond the reach of pain
    and consciousness of wrong.
    But a living woman
    bullied from joy to sorrow,
    pity her, for she is lost
    to her old self: and every moment of her life
    is raw with knowledge of her loss.
    Her life is like a wound that cannot heal.
    Your dead daughter is like an unborn child.
    Polyxena is dead, knowing nothing
    of the man who killed her
    or of his lust for her.

    It is well for any woman
    to consider the nature of a man's lust.
    I did.

    I noted and considered why men praise women.
    Aware of the reasons for their praise

I did everything to please my man,
Hector. I realised that always,
whatever a woman's motives may be,
straight or twisted, dark or in the light,
innocent or guilty, wrong or right,
to try her hand with another man
puts her immediately in a dubious light.
So I stayed at home and walked in my own garden.
I did not allow into my home
the kind of woman
who delights in giving another woman
a bad name.
The glinting knives of gossiping tongues
never even scratched me.
I thought my own thoughts
and found they were enough.
When Hector came to me
he found me bright and peaceful.
I gave him what his heart desired,
hearing, always what he had to say.
I became a gifted listener, patient, sympathetic.
In my husband's presence,
I had a quiet tongue and a pleasant face.
I understood him, I understood myself,
and so I created a fair, effective way of living;
I knew when to insist
and when to obey.
I never resorted to any evil guile,
I created a life
with my own, deliberate style.
I created the space in which his vanity might move
like a beautiful, confident cat.

I created peace.
And then this peace became my enemy.
The Greek, Achilles' son, hearing of my peace,
chose me.
Now I must serve the killer of my husband.
I must lie in the bed of my husband's murderer.
But how shall I serve such a man?
Shall I forget
my Hector's handsome face

and open up my heart
to this new master?

Shall I betray the dead
whom I was glad to serve?
And how shall I feel
when I am fucked by his murderer
in that murderer's bed?
And if in bed I shrink
from the embrace of this fresh lover
will he beat me, cripple me,
or strike me dead in rage?

After all, I'm only a slave.
If I'm a slave, shall I think like a slave?
And what does that mean — thinking like a slave?

Men who have studied their own lust
will tell you
that a single night in a man's arms
will tame the wildest woman.
Shame! My thoughts begin to shame me.
Can a woman's lips so soon forget
her dead
and quickly love the lust in a stranger's bed?
Who can blame the woman that —
her husband in his grave —
explores the unknown possibilities of love?
Will not a lively mare run on, run on
to another stallion, when her mate is gone?
O my dead Hector, most loved of men
who, all alive, was mine and only mine,
my love, my prince, my man, my perfect majesty,
no man had ever touched me
when you strode masterfully into my life
and masterfully took me for your wife.
And you are dead, Hector, dead
as yesterday's love;
and I must be
a slave and take my chances on the sea
and be the kind of woman
that a man will say I have to be.
And yet I clearly see

that if my body is a slave
an untouched portion of my mind is free.
To be a slave and free at once – how can this be?
I am a woman; men will put me on the sea.
And yet, no matter where I am, I still must think of me.

What does dead Polyxena
for whom you weep
know of the twists and turns of her own mind? Nothing!
What does she know of mad frantic inexplicable dreams
that leave her mind and body
exhausted in the light of dawn?
Nothing! Nor does she need to know.
My mind is crookeder and wilder
than any dream I've ever had.
I have no hope; I know I have no hope.
Nor will I lie to myself in my private hell
pretending that my plight is well,
or fairly well.
And yet, I dream. Some dreams are sweet,
even a slave will dream. Somewhere, a special light
burns for me, for you, for all lost women...
A good dream to a slave
is a crust of bread to a starving beggar.
Better a good dream than a futile pain in the heart.

FIRST WOMAN. You have already gone where I must go.
You know completely what I must try to know.

HECUBA. Look at the ships.
I have heard that when a storm comes
each man does his best to face it
and if the sea wins
the men surrender
to the conquering storm.
I surrender to my own grief,
I don't struggle, I don't curse the sea
or strive to make things be
other than the way they have to be.
Over me they pour, the waves, great waves of misery.

God's overwhelming waves are drowning me!
My child, let Hector sleep.

You may weep
till the eyes melt from your head.
Your weeping will not bring him from the dead.
Keep the unstained beauty of your eyes
for the man you'll sleep with soon.
Be gentle, modest, dutiful and wise
and win this man. Be a winner, Andromache.
Go eagerly to bed with this new man
and let your body teach
you how to win.
When you let him lose himself in you,
there's nothing that you cannot gain.
He thinks you're his slave;
you know he's yours.
Now, you have your master in your power,
help those who love you and whom you love.
Your conqueror is conquered by your guile,
he cannot distinguish his own fulfilment from your style.
The poor, blind winner!
Rear this child among your enemies,
Hector's child, that he may grow
among his enemies in mastery
and hope and strength. One day,
he'll help again, when stone on stone is laid,
to build a city that will restore our pride
and our own loved ways of living.
O how my mind is leaping, leaping,
thought chasing thought like athletes running
before the cheering people on a summer's evening.
My thoughts are swifter now
than any sword flashing in a man's hand!
But who is this?
Talthybius! Again, Talthybius!

Enter TALTHYBIUS *with soldiers. He's upset.*

TALTHYBIUS. Andromache! Hector's wife!
     Brave wife of the bravest man in Troy,
     I have no joy in telling you this.
     The people and the Kings have all agreed to...

ANDROMACHE. There's evil on your lips.
     Speak it.

TALTHYBIUS. Your child –

ANDROMACHE. Yes?

TALTHYBIUS. Your son will never see you
    serve another man;
    your son's voice will never speak
    in obedience to a Greek.

ANDROMACHE. Good!
    Will they leave him here
    to re-build this old city
    of his father, mother, sisters, brothers,
    ancestors?

TALTHYBIUS. The people...the Kings...

ANDROMACHE. If you have bad news to tell,
    tell it now. Why can't you speak? Why? Speak!

TALTHYBIUS. Your son must die.

ANDROMACHE. I can sleep in my enemy's bed.
    But my son – dead!
    My son – murdered by the Greeks.
    Dead!

TALTHYBIUS. Odysseus, speaking before everyone,
    argued eloquently that –

ANDROMACHE. Lost! My son! My city! Lost!

TALTHYBIUS. Odysseus argued and Odysseus won.
    He said that the son of Hector,
    the son of one so brave and threatening
    should not be allowed to grow to manhood –

ANDROMACHE. May his own words
    curse the lives of his own sons.
    May they never grow to men
    but be forever
    dead, forgotten boys.
    May Odysseus be cursed forever.

TALTHYBIUS. Odysseus argued and Odysseus won.
    He said your boy must be flung
    from the topmost heights

of the walls of Troy.
Let it be done – now.
No waiting! No thinking!
You are a brave woman in great pain,
do not look for strength no man or God
can give you.
Look around you here.
Is there hope or help or refuge anywhere?
Your city is taken
your man is dead
you are alone and weak, a woman alone,
a prisoner alone, one woman, a slave.
How can you resist or fight
or struggle for even a moment?
I beg you, Andromache, do not struggle,
I do not want to see you hurt
Or wounded, your blood among the stones...

Why are your lips
moving in silence? Are you cursing the ships
and every Greek they bear?
If I hear one evil word from you
your son will get no burial
but be flung broken and naked –
O my God! Peace!
Andromache! Peace!
Bear this misfortune as you have borne
all your troubles.
This is war, woman. You must live with war
and the terrible consequences of war,
live with war, bear it and bury your child.
If you learn to live with this
no Greek will deepen your loss.
They will recognise your courage.
Andromache, this boy must be flung from the battlements.

ANDROMACHE. You must die, my child,
    you must die at the hands of pitiless men,
    leaving me alone.
    Your father was too brave:
    that's why the Greeks are killing you.
    His bravery was such

the Greeks fear it in you. They know
that while you live your father is not dead.
Your father's bravery saved the lives of others.
Now, it is the cause of your death.
If you live...you are your father.
O my son, my son!
Kiss me, my son!

The sea...the city in my head.
O God! When I went to Hector's bed
I was a girl in love with a brave man,
brave enough to challenge the world
and the bravest in it. I have no art,
no language to speak of your dead father's
bravery of heart.
There was no end to his daring...
My son, why are you crying?
Why? Why? You cannot know your father.
Your father will not come
your father will not come
not once, not even once,
his sword splitting the grave itself
to set you free.
No, my son, your father will not come.

Your death? How will it happen?
The Greeks will throw you from the city walls.
Down, down through the air
that brought sweet life to our city and its people,
down through the air you'll plunge –
my God, your body, my son's body,
your back, your head, your neck,
your neck that I have kissed
and kissed and touched and lingered over –
and there's no pity!
And is it for nothing, nothing at all
that I have reared you?
Is it to see your body
pitched from a great height
to break on the earth
that I nursed you through long sickness,
watching over you till I felt

old and withered with watching,
my head falling in unwilling sleep,
forcing myself awake
that I might not miss one moment watching you.
Kiss me, my son
kiss me once
and never again.
Put your arms about my neck,
my son, my brave Hector's son,
your arms about my neck
and kiss me, kiss me, your lips
into my lips –
You Greeks,
you are torturing me
as no woman has ever been tortured.
A child, why murder a child,
an innocent child? And will I witness it?

At the back of all this – a woman.
Helen, may every curse
that ever issued
from the mind of God and man
blast and savage your heart
and every part of your body
until the rats and vampires of the world
fear to come near you.
May sickness and disease
scar and madden your beautiful eyes
and may your name be hated by children
until the world howls
to its miserable end.
Helen, you are not human.
You are the daughter of many fathers,
evil, hate, murder, death,
every monster prowling the earth.
Helen, you are killing my son.
in your lovely eyes
I see my son falling to his death.

(She gives her son to TALTHYBIUS.*)*

Quick! Take him! Drag him to the wall!
Throw him from the highest point!

Smash him in such pieces
I cannot recognise him.
Men, beasts, take him, break him,
be quick, this is war, be quick,
live with war, be quick, see, I do not resist,
I am more impotent than any old man,
I am a helpless woman, woman alone, alone.
Throw him, crack flesh, break bone,
I cannot lift a hand to help the boy,
throw me from the highest wall,
scatter me under the ships,
my coward's body will disgust the sea.

(She faints, half-rises, then −)

Quick! I must go to a Greek's bed!
My son is dead, this is war,
there must be love somewhere. Dead.

The soldiers close around her.

FIRST WOMAN. For Helen's kiss,
for one vile woman's kiss
we have come to this!
Thousands of young men are dead
because of one woman's hateful bed.
Helen! Is Helen human?

TALTHYBIUS *bends over her and takes the child from her.*

TALTHYBIUS. Child, let your mother go.
Come with me
to the towering walls above
your father's city.

There you will meet your death
− Hold! Hold him! Hold him tight! −
Why must I, who love child-brightness,
quench this light?

Why must I end a life
that has hardly begun?
Why must I kill an innocent
when the war is won?

Would to heaven some other man

did what I must do.
To kill a child! Is this my glory?
No more! Do it! Now!

HECUBA. Child, you are my son's son
and these Greeks are killing you.
They have stripped me of everything.
What can I offer you?

Take my battered heart,
take my beaten head,
these are the gifts I offer you
on your way to the dead, .

the last gifts in my power to give.
Nothing lives but pain.
As long as I breathe I will say this
again and again –

Our city is a city of pain
our days are days of pain
Is there any end to human pain?
Are there any words for the final pain?
(She breaks down.)

The child breaks free from TALTHYBIUS, *starts back to his mother, is
grabbed by a soldier.* ANDROMACHE *is dragged off to the ships – cries
of 'To the ships! To the ships! – and* TALTHYBIUS *takes the child.*

WOMAN. A child is taken to his death,
a woman dragged to shame.
That's how a city dies.

Silent houses break up inside.
Ships' bellies are crammed with women.
That's how a city dies.

Who has time for broken things?
Or ghosts? Or stories of things done and said
by men and women long with the dead?
That's how a city dies.

Women stolen away by sea
are prizes, prizes –
something no fighting man denies.

And what is love? And where is love?
We have grown so used to murder
we no longer hear the cries.
Love is murdered here today.
That's how a city dies.

King MENELAUS *enters, with soldiers.*

MENELAUS. I cannot imagine a more perfect day!
I am about to see the woman that I –
No, I haven't come here for her.
I came for the man
who ate and drank with me
and stole my woman.
But Paris is long dead
battered to pieces by the hooves
of good Greek horses.
Today I want to see –
Curse the bitch! She was my wife
and I can hardly bring myself
to say her name.
She's with the prisoners here
in one of these huts,
here, among the women-slaves.
The men who fought to win her
have given her to me
to do with as I will. Imagine! As I will!
Shall I take her for pleasure
here, now, right here, even now?
Or pretend to kill her?
And get a little pleasure from her fear?
Or shall I take her home?
Shall I take Helen home?
Home! No, I'll not kill Helen here.
I'll take her home across the sea
and there hand her over to these families
who've lost their young men fighting for her.
They'll think of ways to deal with her.
Soldiers! Go into these huts,
drag out that bitch from where she's crouching
in some stinking corner.
Find her, drag her out here,

pull her by that famous blood-drenched hair
thousands of young Greeks have died for,
and drag her here before me, here,
before my very eyes –

(He controls himself.)

And when a favourable wind will come
my ships will take her home.

The soldiers approach a hut to force the door, second hut on the left.

HECUBA. Whoever you are,
    ruler of every star and every river
    beat of every creature's heart
    maker and sustainer of all living things
    the blood that courses and the voice that sings
    of dreams born in solitude,
    God,
    I praise you now with all my being,
    seeing
    that justice strides into our midst
    when all seemed lost.

MENELAUS. That is a strange prayer.
    (Turning.) Who spoke these words to heaven?

HECUBA. Do not look long in Helen's eyes.
    If you look into her eyes
    you will drown
    as surely as a drunken man
    staggering alone at night
    through a treacherous swamp will drown
    in the sneering light of the moon.
    If you look into her eyes
    and surrender to what you see
    or think you see
    you will forget who you are
    and the purpose of your coming here.
    Your anger will seem strange to you.
    You will no longer feel the need for vengeance.
    You will not be then
    the man you are now.
    If you look deep in Helen's eyes
    your sense of yourself

will melt like a candle
in the depth of night.
And what use is a melted self,
a helpless lump of wax that Helen
using her old magical skill
will shape, manipulate according to her will?
She traps strong men
she poisons homes
she steals men's hearts
she snares great cities
she is a cup of magic;
drink it
you will drown in her,
you are hers forever,
lost to yourself
trapped in adoration of her eyes,
her lips, her face, her hair,
yes, you will find Helen here.
Do I not know her?
Do you not know her?
All these, do they not know her
the eloquent, evil, beautiful Queen
of all that women know to be obscene
and men cannot, will not, or refuse to recognise?

The soldiers return with HELEN, *gentle, composed, unafraid.*

HECUBA. Menelaus, when you look in Helen's eyes,
Think of her victims!

MENELAUS. You are my prize.

HECUBA. Listen to her, Menelaus. Hear her out
and when she has spoken
let me answer.
You know nothing of the wrongs and horrors
she unleashed in this city.
Hear her story and you'll know why
this cool, manipulating bitch must die.
But as you listen to her story, beware of her tongue.

MENELAUS. Helen's story! A waste of breath and time
and yet for your sake, Hecuba, I'll hear her out.
I have no mercy for her, but let her speak!

HELEN. (*Points to* HECUBA.) Blame this woman!
This woman started it all!
She gave birth to Paris,
the man who stole me from you.
Out of her womb sneaked the thief
of your happiness.
Before the birth, Hecuba dreamed
she had a firebrand in her womb.
She knew she was the mother of destruction.

Look at her now!
Shall we call her a woman?
Or a tyrant judge, rigid with accusation,
lusting for my blood?
Or a twisted bitter jealous thing
poisoned by memory?
Or a bad lump of envy
raging for lost beauty?
Who is this woman
who cannot wait to scream for my death?

Why did I leave you, Menelaus?
I was stolen by Paris, the firebrand in her womb.
Paris saw me, loved me, stole me away.
For my beauty I was captured
and brought across the sea.
Do not blame me for my beauty.
My beauty should have been the reason
why my people love me
as I loved you, a reasonable man.

But why did I leave you, Menelaus?
Why did I run away with another man?
Paris came, Paris the firebrand came,
a goddess came with him, with Paris
whom you welcomed to your house
and left alone with me.
You left me alone with a firebrand!
Remember that
when it comes to handing out the blame.
Blame! Hecuba blames me
for the evil she launched on the world,
she blames me for her misery.

These other women blame me for theirs.
Yet Hecuba and all these women
encouraged their men to fight
and when they lost
they pitched their blame on me.

There must always be someone to blame, Menelaus.
At home, men and women blame me for their dead,
for all the young men lost in this long war.
Why do they go to war?
They go to war to fuck each other to death
and then the daisies sprout laughing from their corpses.
The mad absurdity of it all!
Tens of thousands play war's murderous game
and when the game is over
and the dead must be buried,
the maimed and crippled comforted,
the women chosen for the winners' beds,
someone must be blamed
for what had to happen
because men must sink their swords
in the backs and bellies of other men.
Think, Menelaus, think!
Your knife is deep in the flesh of another man,
he's screaming, screaming,
your knife goes deeper,
deeper than you've ever been in any woman,
deeper than you've ever been in me.
Listen! His screams are changing,
becoming whispers,
your knife is cutting the throats of fear and shame.
No, Menelaus, no! I am not to blame!

You left Paris alone with me
and took to the open sea,
away from me, away, away from me,
leaving Paris alone with me.

Do you know what it means to be alone?
Alone as a mad woman
who in her madness
has moments when she knows she is not mad?
Alone as a cry for help too obvious to be heard?

Alone as a whisper in a sick room?
Would you rather go to war
than be alone?
Would you rather sink your sword
in the back or belly of another man?
Menelaus, are you grateful to your God
for the mad spilling of young men's blood?
Blood, Menelaus, blood and the screams of the dying
are preferable to the silent screams of being alone.

You are far away from me now,
lost at the other side of the sea.
Have you ever looked at me,
praised me,
touched me?
I am here, I think my own strange thoughts,
stranger than the screams of the dying
or the murderous lust of the living,
the obscene obviousness of war?
Would you like to look into my mind
and surprise yourself with what you find?
You know my body, Menelaus; now I offer you my mind
where I find this question: why did I forget
my love, my land, my family and friends
to sail the sea with a strange man?

Surely it was not I,
not I alone (how should I ever dare?)
but the goddess standing at Paris's side
that prompted me to go!

Surely it was not I, but she.
If you must punish anyone
for the fact that I am here
and not at home with you, my Lord,
then punish her who prompted him
who prompted me to run away
from all that I held dear.
Yes, I did wrong
but I did wrong because of her.

I am not to blame.

You know my body, Menelaus.

Here is my mind again.
This is your question: why,
when Paris at last was dead and buried,
and I was freed from the spell
cast by the goddess,
why did I still stay in his house?
Why did I not escape to the Greek ships
and be safe among my own people,
be with you, dear Menelaus? Alone with you?

I tried, I tried,
so many times I tried, but all in vain!
That old gate-guardian was the man
who thwarted every attempt I made
to reach the ships. I was watched,
Menelaus, watched night and day.
Day and night I plotted my escape,
waiting always for the golden moment.
It never came. The guards and sentinels
knew of my intention to escape
and more than once they tied me to a rope
and dangled me from the battlements.
But still I kept my hope
that one day I'd escape
and go where I belonged:
in your house, Menelaus, in your gracious house.
Alone with you, Menelaus.

My husband, you have heard my story.
How can you kill me
who never meant you a moment's harm?
Calm the storm in your mind.
Think quietly. Listen!
I was stolen from you.
I did not leave you.
I suffered misery and pain
at the hands of a strange man.

I use my own words
to speak my own truth.

If you choose to kill me for my truth
then kill me: but know

it is Helen's truth you kill
to your eternal shame.
Truth-killer Menelaus – may that never be your name.
Your name is sweeter far than that,
Menelaus, reasonable man, lover of justice,
patient listener to a pleading voice,
Helen's voice,
Helen who loved you truly
in your own house.

MENELAUS. Thousands of young men are dead –
and you are not to blame?

HELEN. No! I am not to blame!
As Helen is my name
I swear to heaven I am not to blame!
What did any single one
of all these thousands of young men who died
know of *me*?
That war was fought
in furious ignorance by ignorant men!
Not one, not one who died, knew *me*!

They knew as much of me
as they did of whatever lives or dies
at the bottom of the sea!
And why must you blame me, my beauty,
my leaving your bed for another man?
Why blame me
for your own pride, your own bafflement,
your need to own me?
Nobody owns me.
Do not blame me, Menelaus,
love me for my truth.
Look into my eyes,
listen to my voice,
we are together again, we are living
together in the warm house of our love.
Look into my eyes
listen to my voice
this is my skin, my flesh, my face, my hair.
These are my hands, reaching out to you forever.
Touch me, touch me, there, there...

Touch me, you will recover everything you've lost.
Touch me, you will know again the man you really are.
When you touch me, you are following your true star.

WOMAN. Break her spell, Hecuba, break her spell!
Her voice is heaven but her heart is hell.
She is eloquent, evil, beautiful, vile!
She makes me so afraid! Break her spell!

HECUBA. Helen is a liar! She lives to lie!
Lies spring more quickly from her lips
than evil glances from a demon's eye.
Helen has lied her way through life
and cannot cease to lie until she dies.
Everything within her and about her
is a lie. The greatest lie of all
is her beauty. She uses it to get her way.
That is Helen's truth – getting her way!
That's why she blames a goddess
for her own icy lust
as men blame God
for their own pathetic failures.
Outrageous, smiling, lying bitch!
Getting your way through lies!
Do you think you have the power
to deceive not only Menelaus,
not only me, Hecuba,
but all of us women
who have seen you fawning for years,
smiling, cheating, lying, deceiving for years,
getting your way
with beauty and with style.

My God! The hideous simplicity
of complex women!

My son was beautiful.
Paris was a handsome prince of a man.
You didn't have to look at him twice,
Helen, to know that.
Beauty has an eye for beauty.
Your beauty hides the mind
of a manipulating bitch, the kind of bitch

men trample on each other to get near,
the kind of low bitch
who must be always at the top.
In you, Helen, the stink of evil
is a personal perfume.
When you saw Paris
your lying heart began its charming war.
First, you charmed yourself
and then him.

When you saw his youth and beauty,
his vigorous, magnetic fire,
you wanted him to add to you,
to increase your beauty, deepen your desire,
fire the passion that was dying
in the comfortable house of Menelaus.
You were growing listless, Helen, bored and listless
because you'd got your way with Menelaus.
A bored, beautiful woman is a monster.
You are the most beautiful monster
the world has known.

So Paris took you – by force, of course!
And you were brave, resisting to the end!
Yet no one heard your cries for help!
It was night, I know, and people slept
while you, poor captive, whimpered and wept
for your lost darling Menelaus!

Then when you came to Troy,
and quietly sat among your lovely lies
and men died everywhere for you,
you played it both ways.

One day it was 'Paris, O my love,
O my dear, unequalled man,
no woman dares to love you as I can.'
And the next moment –
'Where is Menelaus?
Where is my loving lord
who understood my every little word?'

How you suffered, Helen!
How your heart split in two

while young men in their thousands
died for you!
But you know that's what men are for:
they fight and work and laugh and sometimes cry.
Pick one, Helen. Pick a man. Fuck him. Let him die.
Stick him in a grave, cold, deep, far from the sun.
And remember always – take care of number one.
Remember when I tried to help you escape?
I said, 'I will get you back to your own people
and my people will have peace at last,'
and you replied that I was talking like a traitor,
like an enemy of my own people.

And you were concerned for my people!
Why not?
Servants tended you, bowed to you,
your every whim was satisfied,
every wish granted,
every lie swallowed as a child
will swallow promises.

And now, you come out here,
brazen-beautiful as ever,
you dare to stand there
in my presence, before my eyes
and – I can't believe it! – spin your lies
to get your way.
How can such evil
have such a perfect style?

You should have crawled out here
like the beast you are
dressed in the stinking rags and tatters
that show your heart.
You should be trembling here,
your head should be cropped of that hair,
you should know yourself for the guilty thing you are.
But no, you are Helen still, and therefore
a liar to the end!
Helen, you are whatever
turns a man into a murderer,
you created the thought of rape,
you are the cause of all our torture
and you will not escape!

King Menelaus, it's time for justice.
Kill her!
Kill her and let others live.
Think of what she said, of what I've said.
Now is the time for justice
for the woman who betrayed your bed.
Kill her, now! Now!
Be urgent as you are wise.
Kill her! Then make a law for women everywhere:
Whatever woman betrays her husband, dies!

HELEN. (*To* HECUBA.) You look at me as if you'd never seen
a woman in your life.

HECUBA. Yes. A woman. But what do I see in you?

HELEN. What do you see?

HECUBA. I see a cunt. I see an evil cunt.
It's all you are. Your answer to everything.
The only thing you have to offer to the world.
You use what you are to be more than you are.
Men exist to help you do that.

HELEN. What else do you see?

HECUBA. I see a greedy, scheming bitch
who wants to take, take, take
till she's grabbed everything and everybody
for herself.

HELEN. What else do you see?

HECUBA. I see a traitor, not only of men
but of women.
Treachery is written on your skin.

HELEN. What else do you see?

HECUBA. I see an animal that knows when to strike and kill,
that knows also when to be passive
and slink away into the silence of herself.

HELEN. What else do you see?

HECUBA. I see a woman who can act
whatever part she chooses.
We women play one part, one part alone.

The circling women become more and more enraged. They throw insults like stones at HELEN.

WOMEN *circling, shout and scream the following:*

> Thousands of young men dead!
> Homes destroyed!
> Families broken!
> Blood spilled!
> Broken bodies!
> Broken minds!
> Broken hearts.
> You broke them!
> You broke the homes!
> You killed the young men!
> You gave your body to get your way!
> You cheated!
> Lied!
> Stole!
> Left one man for another!
> You wanted everything!
> Everything! For yourself!
> You're an insult to women!
> You mock what we are!
> You're a disgrace!
> A shame!
> Traitor!
> Double-dealer!
> Schemer!
> Nothing matters to you!
> Except what pleases you!
> Scum!
> Trash!
> Swamp!
> Shit!
> Muck!
> Pricktease!
> Wagon!
> Cocksucker!
> Cow!
> Sow!
> Vixen!
> Hustler!

Tart!
Trollop!
Hussy!
Doxy!
Minx!
Rotten fish!
Bag o' crap!
Witch!
Bitch!
Whore!
Slave!

HECUBA. Cunt!

WOMAN. Death to Helen!
Death to the traitor!
King Menelaus, let your judgement
be fair and strong.
It's clear to all the world
Helen has done a dreadful wrong
but it would be a far more dreadful wrong
to let her live!
Kill her! Kill her!

The other women continue to circle HELEN, *hissing-chanting 'Kill her!
Kill her!' During all this,* HELEN *remains calm.*

MENELAUS. (*Turns furiously on* HELEN.)
Get out of here! Men and women
are waiting for you with stones.
You made corpses of their sons,
you filled their hearts with skeletons.
These men and women,
face their hate and rage on every road,
at every window, every door;
and when your body's broken by the stones of hate
you will dishonour me no more.
Get out! You fooled me for too long.
You cannot reach me with your lying tongue.

HELEN. (*Kneels before him, embraces him.*)
I wrap my arms about your knees
as I was happy to embrace your body
and will be happy, if you wish, again.

Judge me for who I am.
Helen, your Helen, Helen is who I am, nobody but Helen,
remember that. How can you kill me?

HECUBA. Remember the young men she murdered,
young men who fought at your side,
deception is the blood in her body.
Remember that body in another's bed.
If you don't kill her now
and put that body beyond the bodies of men
you'll be her victim once again.
As long as Helen breathes,
Helen will deceive.

MENELAUS. Peace, Hecuba, peace!
If I do not kill her now
it's not for her sake.
Helen is nothing to me,
nothing...almost nothing.

(*To the soldiers.*) Take her to the shore.
Prepare a ship for her.
She's ready for the sea.

HECUBA. Don't go in the same ship with her.

MENELAUS. Why?

HECUBA. No man who has ever loved Helen
can be sure he will not do so again.
Her evil magic never fails with men.

MENELAUS. Let some other ship take her then.
When we reach home
she will be welcomed by her doom,
black doom, black as her heart.
When women see what Helen must endure
they will be faithful for evermore.
This will not be easy
but the sight of Helen in her blood,
her body bruised and broken
in shreds of meat a man might throw to dogs
will freeze the wandering dreams of women
and keep them in the beds where they belong.
Helen's body, gashed and hacked by stones,

will chill the marrow of the wildest women's bones.
The sight of Helen's blood will do some good,
the body of this vile whore will please the eyes of God.

Exit MENELAUS, *after* HELEN, *escorted by soldiers.*

HECUBA. Will she live or die?
   Will she sink in shame and pain
   or will the old magic work again?
   What does she *do* to men?
   What demon helps her to get her way
   and yet make men believe her only wish
   is to do as they say?
   Her style, the gift of hell,
   twists men to her design
   and yet persuades them all is well,
   as if she really is what she but seems.
   She makes men feel she is their slave
   but she remains the queen of all their dreams.

WOMAN. Laughter is dead as our nights of joy,
   the passion of every blessing and every prayer,
   the towers and houses, the bread of Troy
   the moons of love and hope in the air.
   My heart cries, God of the tolerant sky
   what did we ever mean in your mind?
   Our fabulous city, about to die.
   Our people, all, dead leaves in the wind.

HECUBA. Give the dead a chance.

WOMAN. My man is dead.
   I go to the long ships,
   a stranger's bed
   a stranger's lips.

HECUBA. These lips will bring you hope
   if you listen to everything they say.
   Listen! Listen! And you'll find a way.
   Learn from your oppressor!

WOMAN. My children cry for me,
   but I must go from them forever.
   Where? Where beyond the sea?
   What city? Village? Town?

Who will sleep with me?
What sort of man
waits for me out there?
Is his heart cruel or kind?
Will he set my mind at ease?
Will he drive me out of my mind?
Will I wander here and there
calling my children's names aloud?
How long will they remember me?
Or will the morning dawn at last
when they won't give a thought to me?
I cannot forget my past.
I'll take it with me on the sea!

HECUBA. The past is richness and waste.

WOMAN. Far out in the waste of the sea
where as a slave I go
I ask one favour of you,
God whom I do not know –
Strike me dead on that sea
where my master's arrogant breath
offends me and strengthens my prayer
for the gift of death.

WOMAN. I have failed! I have failed!

HECUBA. You have not failed!
There is no such thing as failure!
There's only something that you haven't learned,
something that you cannot see.

WOMAN. May I see Helen there,
the blight of all our lives,
may vermin infest her hair,
may the curses of daughters and wives
wither her hands and face.
May poison shrivel her guts
may she never know one hour's peace
from the busy teeth of rats.
May the cold of death assail her
and every pain known to man,
may her womb blacken with cancer
and cancer eat her brain

till she staggers, a reeling idiot
from bed to rutting bed
with lovers whose touch is leprosy
whose flesh is both lusty and dead.

Enter TALTHYBIUS, *one or two soldiers,* TALTHYBIUS *carrying the dead child,* ASTYNAX.

WOMAN. A dead boy.
Is there no end to the misery of Troy?

TALTHYBIUS. Andromache is gone, her master's prize:
Andromache who brought tears to my eyes
with her words about her country,
her city and her man, Hector.
She asked me that her son be buried
with proper rites.
Here is Hector's shield.
Andromache requested
that this shield cover her son's body.
She asked me to place the boy
in your hands, Hecuba.
Let him be dressed in whatever clothes
are left to you.
She cannot do these things herself.
Her master won't allow it.
From now on,
she has no choices of her own.
As soon as the boy's body is dressed
we will bury him in the earth
and then set sail.
Do this quickly,
let there be no delay,
quickly, as you've been told.
One thing you need not do, however.
Some distance back I passed a river,
I washed the body in the water,
I cleaned his wounds...
a boy's body...

I will go out now and dig his grave.
Go, do your work, dress the body
and return immediately.

Then, at last, I will be free
to make my way to the waiting sea.
Go.

He goes out with soldiers, leaving the boy's body in HECUBA'*s arms.*

HECUBA. Put Hector's great shield here,
near me, on the ground.
Look at it. The Greeks knew fear
whenever they saw that shield,
wielded by the bravest man of all.
Did Hector ever murder a child?
It takes a Greek to do that.
Even for Greeks, this was a strange murder.
Why were they so afraid
that one day this boy might restore
his country's pride?
We are beaten, lashed, smashed into the ground,
our men are dead, our women slaves,
our city burnt, our fields destroyed,
our hearts broken, our bodies weary –
and the Greeks murder a boy!

Is innocence to be more feared
than strength?
What a death they gave you, boy!
If you had grown
and fought and fallen like a man
then we could have spoken of you
as we do of the blessèd dead.
Your eyes saw the world
you breathed the good air
you did not get the chance to live
the full, rich life that was your due.

Thrown from the walls of your own city!

Broken! All broken!

Your head, your hands, shoulders, neck:
broken.
So this is it, the end of all:
a child's crushed skull!
Death grins out of your face!

I watched over you in sleep.
I played with you,
the daft and giddy games you loved.
I fell asleep with you,
I woke and looked at you.
We played again.

Grown men feared you!
Ah! The stupid, murderous fear of grown men!

Child, there's nothing left in Hector's house,
nothing left but Hector's shield.
It will cover your body.
Your father's hand gripped that shield
and he was feared.
Now it will cover you
with all we know of love.

(*To the women.*) Go, bring whatever clothes remain.
I am sorry I have so little to give you
and yet I give you all I can.
How vain, how vain are men
who rob and plunder
and think they'll always be
rulers of the land and of the sea.
Vain men! Vain men!
O my broken child of Troy!

Women approach with flowers and clothes.

WOMAN. These women have taken clothes from their dead
  to dress the boy's body.

During the following scene, HECUBA *gradually takes the clothes and wraps
the child.*

HECUBA. I dress you for your burial
  with the same love I dressed you,
  living, for your play.
  My son's son, I love you more
  than I can say.

  Helen! You killed this boy.
  How shall you escape your punishment?
  If I could lay my hands on you now
  I'd rip your flesh to pieces

shred by evil shred.
Because of your whorish lust
my son's son will break in dust.
He's ready for the dead!

Your father's shield!
Lie under it! Lie still!
A part of me is glad to know
you never learned how to kill.

Men kill! They kill! They kill!
They never learn! They're stupid still!
I know war's stupid, they call it glory.
The lie endures, they call it history.

They strut and preen and swell with pride
and you are dead; and you are dead
and captive women will breed and die
while under your father' shield you lie.

FIRST WOMAN. The decent earth is waiting for the boy,
decent and peaceful at the end of all,
our most patient mother.

SECOND WOMAN. Peaceful and decent and calm and strong.

THIRD WOMAN. And witnessing the infinite wrong!

(HECUBA *has been performing funeral rites, symbolically staunching the wounds.*)

HECUBA. Broken thing, I'd make you whole again
to live and play, to enjoy this mad world of men.
I touch this wound, and this, and this;
I still dream of your happiness.
You're standing at a door in evening light,
you are twenty years of age, the world is opening
like a flower, a morning, an idea, a story
and you are going to...
Your burial rite!
Let it be spoken!
Leave me!
Go to your father!
(Bows her head, motionless, sees nothing.)

WOMAN. If I could,
I'd take your grief on my own head.

HECUBA. Women, good women!
    Myself! My own!
    (She gets up, looks bewildered as if she'd had a vision.)

WOMAN. Yes, we are yours.
    We are with you.

HECUBA. I stood before the face of God
    and looked into his open hand.
    His hand contained nothing,
    only the black seeds of our destruction,
    small black vital seeds in the hand of God.
    I saw all our prayers
    blown around his head
    like dust in the wind.
    If he reached out
    he couldn't catch the dust.
    The dust of all our prayers
    will blow beyond
    every known and unknown sea.
    And then I saw us all,
    us women who must bear
    the murderous consequences of war,
    I saw us all
    gathered in God's hand.
    And is he kind?
    He turned us in his hand
    he ruined what we cherished
    crumbled our houses
    shook our squares and streets
    brought low our hopes
    made our hills tremble
    like children before bullies

    until we knew that we had suffered
    the most unspeakable wrong.

    And then amid the dust, amid the wrong,
    amid the trembling hills and cities
    amid the streets of rubble and the fields of death

    I heard the music of our hearts
    I knew the everlasting beauty of the song
    of earth and heaven.

I kissed God's hand! I am real. I am so real
I am not afraid to look into the eyes of God.

(*To the women.*) Bury him!
Clean his grave as best you can,
let him rot into reality!
We living have our dreams, our vanity.

*The women take the body on the shield. Flames begin to rise from the
city. Forms, shadows in the flames.*

TALTHYBIUS. *(Comes out through the broken wall.)*
Burn everything in sight.
Burn everything until all this
is a huge, black, ashen circle
where a future man may stand and say
'There was a city here once!
People lived here! I don't believe it!'
Burn everything until there is no past.
Think of this city as an evil woman,
set fire to her flesh, her hair
rip our her heart, set fire to that,
stand back, enjoy the flames,
this is the best work you've ever done.

And ye – women – stand here
until you hear the trumpet call.
You'll hear it over every ruined wall
and when you do, go forward
to the ships.

And you, Hecuba; follow!
Odysseus has sent his men
to take you. Forget your dead!
Prepare your mind and body for a special bed!

HECUBA. You intend to destroy everything? Everything?

TALTHYBIUS. I am a go-between.
I know the two sides of this story.
I know that if anyone here, anyone,
man, woman, girl, boy,
has even the faintest seed of hope
in the farthest corner of his heart
all this work may go for nothing.

70

The work and purpose of my life is to destroy
everything that you hold dear,
every final seed of hope
you carry in your heart.
There's nothing more dangerous to a winner
than one seed of hope in the heart of the loser.
That's why everything must be destroyed.
You know what I'm saying.
I must kill your hope, Hecuba,
I am killing all your hope.

HECUBA. Are you?
Is this the death of hope?
The meaning of my life?
My city! Fire! Flower!
My flower of hope on fire!

Let me stand here
And look at my city on fire.

My city! You are a woman
eaten by fire!

That fire! It should be eating me!

I will go into the fire!

She goes toward the fire. The soldiers grab her.

TALTHYBIUS. Back!
Hold her for Odysseus.
Hold her!

I have never seen a spirit
To equal hers.

Hold her! Odysseus wants her!
Odysseus will have her!

WOMAN. We are women; we are children too.
What will we do?
Who will help us now?

FIRST WOMAN. God sees all this.
He has no pity.
Heartless, above us all, he watches
The burning and the shaming
and the raping of our city.

Heartless! Heartless!

SECOND WOMAN. I was reared there.
I knew first love there.
I tasted loss there.
I had children there.

Fire! All fire!

THIRD WOMAN. Smoke from the city on fire
rises and scatters.
Smoke is the lives of our men,
our sons and our daughters.
Smoke rises and scatters, pointless and free,
drifting over the sea.

HECUBA *kneels or falls and beats the earth with her hands.*

HECUBA. Earth, you are the mother of my children.
Let them hear my crying.
Children! Your hearts are listening,
there in the darkness lying.
Listen! Listen to me!

WOMAN. Hecuba is praying to the earth
and to the dead!

HECUBA. Listen! I pray again
to every buried shred of flesh and bone,
to every heart. Come near! Come near!
Come into my heart.
Live there, my dead father, mother, husband, sons,
live there, O my dead, as only you can live,
haunt every corner of my blood,
pour through me like a river
through a dying land.

WOMAN. I am near you, Hecuba, near you.
I hear you pray to your dead.
I am near you.
Let me pray to my dead.
My husband, hear my cry.

HECUBA. The dead are not the past, the dead are the future.
They listen and watch, their eyes
like glittering jewels
in the dark streets of eternity!

Listen, you dead!
I am a slave, Hecuba is a slave,
I must go to Odysseus, sleep with him.
I'd rather sleep with a giant rat.

Listen to that!

O my husband, listen to that!
Safe in your nothingness,
homeless and womanless,
know what I feel,
know what I am
in the hands of this man.

Look on my shame!
Do you know what it means
to suffer this?

Do you know? Answer, my husband!

Do you know? Answer, my husband!
Do you know what it means
to have this arrogant trickster, Odysseus,
play tricks with my body,
prowl through every secret of my body
like a smug conqueror exploring
the streets and laneways of a beautiful city?
Do you know what it means for me
to be abandoned by the man I loved,
to have his sympathy replaced by brute silence?
Speak to me! Answer me!
You have no right to silence!
An arrogant, tricky rat of a man claims me
and you are silent!
(HECUBA *beats the earth with her hands.*)

Damn you! Damn your silence! Damn your safe grave!
A man sends his messenger to me
to tell me I am his prize,
and I must go to him.
That man does not know or care who I am.
Who am I? I am a woman,
I am Hecuba, Hecuba, nobody but Hecuba,
I am not a prize, I am not a slave, not a slave
to anyone living or dead,

I am not a decoration or an ornament,
I am not a bit of scandal or a piece of gossip,
I am not something to be shown off or pointed at,
I am not something to be used at someone's beck and call,
I am not a thing, I am not a fuck,
I am telling you who I am,
I am telling you about the man
who is violating every last shred of my dignity,
whose every word is an insult to me
who wants me for his slave
who will have me in his bed.

(She beats the earth in rage, trying to make an impossible link.)

Answer me!
Answer me! You safe, cowardly, silent, blind, buried
bastard of a husband!
Let me hear your voice
through the earth and the grass and the stones.
Tell me what you think
of this insult I suffer
in the depths of my blood,
in the marrow of my bones.
Do you know what I suffer?
This insult? Do you know?

WOMAN. How can he know?
What can he say?

HECUBA. Let me tell you what has happened.
They have murdered the boy Astynax.
They've set fire to the city.
They have destroyed
everything you lived for, worked for, died for.

WOMAN. The living must forget the dead.
If there were no forgetfulness
who would dare to continue?
Then fire attacks our thought
when we remember that we forgot.
Let the dead rest in peace.
In peace let the dead rot.

HECUBA. Dust and smoke! Smoke and dust!
Nothing, nothing, but yes, yes,

final evidence of Helen's lust.
No curse known
to living or dead
is horrible enough
to fall on Helen's head.

Somewhere, there's a song for her.
A man will write it!
It will celebrate her beauty
and millions unborn will sing it.
The man who makes the song
will be so blinded by the blood of war,
he'll see nothing in the darkness of his mind
but Helen's beauty.
She is the mother of horror,
the origin of all our evil,
but the song will make her beautiful,
so beautiful
the horror will be forgotten,
forgotten by all except me
and women like me
who've seen the evil in her eyes,
her lips, her hands, her voice.
Beware the song of Helen's beauty!
I am not fooled by songs or plays
or tales or legends
because I have stood there, in the presence of men,
and seen Helen put her eyes to work
as if her eyes were the agents of her will;
I've seen her subtle hands make history
as other women make bread;
I've seen one eloquent movement of her head
turn critical men into worshippers;
I've seen the very air seduced
by magical ripples
of her sweet manipulating voice.
Her voice is her best song,
song of beauty, song of hell!

WOMAN. The smoke has a voice too,
a fat, black, thick, sluggish voice
that will make the sky sick.
What is the smokevoice saying?

A great crash is heard, the wall is lost in darkness.

WOMAN. Gone! All gone!

HECUBA. All around us, there are men.
>Men fought the war,
>destroyed the city,
>chose us, set us apart,
>decided we are prizes,
>arranged our destinies.
>Men wasted the land.
>Men wait on the sea.
>Men wait in the land beyond the sea.
>And we must go into our future
>as into a dark room.
>Alone in that darkness,
>out of mind, out of sight,
>we will think, when we can,
>of what was once
>our City of Light, City of Peace.

WOMAN. Peace? What is peace?

HECUBA. Although men say they fight for peace,
>peace is what they're most afraid of.
>I remember a city, a street, a house.
>I lived in peace there,
>peace lived in me.
>I loved in peace,
>gave birth in peace,
>reared my children in peace.
>Then she came
>and peace began to die.
>As peace died
>thousands of young men died with it.
>Strange! Peace and youth must always
>die together!
>Peace died in women too
>and yet you ask me, what is peace?
>Peace is the shell of a burnt house,
>peace is a child's body broken in the earth,
>peace is a letter you have read a hundred times,
>a cup or plate or chair or bed
>buried under smoke and dust.

Smoke and dust! Dust and smoke!

(The trumpet sounds.)

Goodbye, goodbye, my city.
Burnt! Lost! Gone!
But still be in me,
be in my blood and in my dreams.

THE WOMEN. Goodbye, goodbye, our city.
Burnt! Lost! Gone!
But still be in us,
be in our blood and in our dreams.

The trumpet sounds again, the women vanish into the dark.

HECUBA. *(Remains standing when the others have gone.)*
There's a man at your side,
there's a man in your mind,
there's a man in your bed:
these men are strangers you've decided to grow used to
because you know them too much, too much.
What are we to make of the strangers
we are to each other and to ourselves?
What does it matter if I sleep with a stranger
here or in another country?
What does it matter if I must
swallow the sour, foul seed
of his vain and suffocating lust?
What does it matter if I fuck
some tricky itchy stinking weasel of a Greek
so long as I know what I'm doing
and why I'm doing it?
And when he's fucking me
may I not smile
and ask the very face of darkness –
darling, who is free?

What does he see? What does he think he sees?
What does he know of me
when he shrinks back into himself, alone,
like a snail shrivelling at my touch,
a man shrivelled with fulfilment,
puny with success, a worm limp with victory,
alone?

Alone,
may I not open or close my eyes,
relishing the part of me that he can never reach,
that no man living can ever reach?
I have a power no man can ever touch.
Although a man may fall asleep at my side,
snoring in fulfilment, fat with vanity,
he'll never dream there is a sea between us.
I can explore that sea
until I find the stranger living in myself
and get to know her and her cold power
as I have never known a man
or permitted any man to know me.
I can walk, talk, think, cry, surprise myself,
I can wonder who I am
and not break apart in madness
because I don't have an answer.
I can look at the rage and hatred in my heart
and know them for what they are –
hatred and rage. Mine!
And I can taste them
as I have tasted love.
I can smell a man
in me, outside me.
I can smell him on my skin,
in the air about me,
and know the kind of stranger that he is.

The darkness deepens. Deep as the sea.
My mind is clear.
What's before me?
The sea! The sea!
Let whatever must happen, happen to me.
I am Hecuba, I am
what life and death have forced me to be.
I know love is a wound and its blood is life.
I have tried to make a space for love.
I have to leave this place. How?
I have to go somewhere. Where?
How shall I go?
I shall put one leg in front of the other
and shuffle towards tonight and tomorrow,

towards a man and his plans,
a man and his fantasy.
One leg in front of the other. So.
That is how I shall reach the sea
and know it for what it is
stretching before me
like all the questions of my life
growing out of each other,
chasing each other
like waves, waves that cannot rest,
like me,
Hecuba, a wave of the sea.

A wave of the sea!
Natural and fearless!
That is what I want –
I want to live without fear
and I will, I will,
no matter where I happen to be,
Hecuba, a woman, Hecuba,
a natural, fearless wave of the sea.

Waves waves waves waves waves
endless unknown driven
dreams in the hearts of women.
Nobody can count the waves,
nobody can count the waves,
the waves tell more
than the waves themselves can ever be,
the waves outnumber every thought
possible to you and me.
The waves roar and moan in pain.
The waves laugh happily.
The waves are slaves.
The waves are free.
The war is over. The war begins – for me!

She goes out slowly.

Brendan Kennelly was born in 1936 in Ballylongford, Co. Kerry, and was educated at St Ita's College, Tarbert, Co. Kerry; at Trinity College, Dublin, where he gained his BA, MA and PhD, and Leeds University. He has lectured in English Literature at Trinity College since 1963, and became its Professor of Modern Literature in 1973. He has also lectured at the University of Antwerp and in America, at Barnard College and Swarthmore College. He has won the AE Memorial Prize for Poetry and the Critics' Special Harveys Award.

He has published more than twenty books of poems, including *My Dark Fathers* (1964), *Collection One: Getting Up Early* (1966), *Good Souls to Survive* (1967), *Dream of a Black Fox* (1968), *Love Cry* (1972), *The Voices* (1973), *Shelley in Dublin* (1974), *A Kind of Trust* (1975), *Islandman* (1977), *A Small Light* (1979) and *The House That Jack Didn't Build* (1982). *The Boats Are Home* (1980) is still available from Gallery Press and *Moloney Up and At It* from the Mercier Press (Cork and Dublin).

He is best-known for two controversial poetry books, *Cromwell*, published in Ireland in 1983 and in Britain by Bloodaxe Books in 1987, and his epic poem *The Book of Judas*, which topped the Irish bestsellers list when it was published by Bloodaxe in 1991.

His books of poems translated from the Irish include *A Drinking Cup* (Allen Figgis, 1970) and *Mary* (Aisling Press, Dublin 1987), and his translations are now collected in *Love of Ireland: Poems from the Irish* (Mercier Press, 1989). He edited *The Penguin Book of Irish Verse* (1970; 2nd edition 1981), and has published two novels, *The Crooked Cross* (1963) and *The Florentines* (1967).

He is also a celebrated dramatist whose plays include versions of *Antigone*, produced at the Peacock Theatre, Dublin, in 1986; *Medea*, premièred in the Dublin Theatre Festival in 1988, toured in England in 1989 by the Medea Theatre Company, broadcast by BBC Radio 3 in 1991 and published by Bloodaxe in 1991; and *The Trojan Women*, first staged at the Peacock Theatre and published by Bloodaxe in 1993. His stage version of *Cromwell* played to packed houses in Dublin and London. His selection *Landmarks of Irish Drama* was published by Methuen in 1988.

His *Journey into Joy: Selected Prose*, edited by Åke Persson, is due from Bloodaxe in 1993, along with *Dublines*, an anthology edited with Katie Donovan.

He has published six volumes of selected poems, most recently *A Time for Voices: Selected Poems 1960-1990* (Bloodaxe, 1990) and *Breathing Spaces: Early Poems* (Bloodaxe, 1992).